SPOTLIGHT ON CIVIC ACTION

BUILDING CONSENSUS

RESPECTING DIFFERENT POINTS OF VIEW

AMANDA MCCULLOCH

PowerKiDS press™

NEW YORK

Published in 2018 by The Rosen Publishing Group, Inc.
29 East 21st Street, New York, NY 10010

Editor: Elizabeth Krajnik
Book Design: Michael Flynn
Interior Layout: Rachel Rising

Photo Credits: Cover, skynesher/ E+/Getty Images; p. 5 iStock.com/Massimo Merlini; p. 6 iStock.com/kali9; p. 7 Iakov Filimonov/Shutterstock.com; p. 9 Svitlana Pimenov/Shutterstock.com; p. 11 iStock.com/monkeybusinessimages; p. 13 Monkey Business Images/Shutterstock.com; p. 15 savitskaya iryna/Shutterstock.com; p. 17 FABRICE COFFRINI/AFP/Getty Images; p. 19 sirtravelalot/Shutterstock.com; p. 21 iStock.com/fstop123; p. 22 asiseeit/E+/Getty Images; p. 23 Syda Productions/Shutterstock.com; p. 25 NICHOLAS KAMM/AFP/Getty Images; p. 27 Bettmann/Bettmann/Getty Images; p. 29 Courtesy of the Library of Congress.

Cataloging-in-Publication Data
Names: McCulloch, Amanda.
Title: Building consensus: respecting different points of view / Amanda McCulloch.
Description: New York : PowerKids Press, 2018. | Series: Spotlight on civic action | Includes index.
Identifiers: ISBN 9781538327869 (pbk.) | ISBN 9781508163930 (library bound) | ISBN 9781538327982 (6 pack)
Subjects: LCSH: Democracy--United States--Juvenile literature. | United States--Politics and government--Juvenile literature. | Consensus (Social sciences) -- United States.
Classification: LCC JK1726.M33 2018 | DDC 320.973--dc23

Manufactured in China

CPSIA Compliance Information: Batch #BW18PK For further information contact Rosen Publishing, New York, New York at 1-800-237-9932.

CONTENTS

MAKING DECISIONS

Consensus means general agreement among all group members in decision-making discussions. The most important part of consensus is that all group members agree to support the decision. We make decisions every day: what clothes we'll wear, what we'll eat for lunch, if we'll walk to school or take the bus. However, these decisions don't need to be made as a group. Some of the decisions we make each day can positively or **negatively** affect the people around us. When making decisions, it is important to be respectful to our peers, and there are a number of ways to make sure of this.

One way to make sure you are treating someone respectfully when talking about a decision is to ask yourself: How would I feel if my opinion wasn't considered? Coming to a consensus means seeing things from the other person's **perspective**.

Some decisions shouldn't be made alone. When it comes to an issue that affects a group of people, the consequences of making a decision without the help of others can cause problems.

WHAT'S THE LAW?

The first thing you should consider when talking about a decision is whether all choices are legal or permitted. For example, you and your group may want some time to work on a project and you want to skip school to complete it. This would be against the rules. While the reason for wanting to skip school seems like a good one, your school principal wouldn't agree. As a group, you need to think about another way to complete the project in time. Perhaps you could work on the project at one person's house after school each day.

Be sure to ask your group members to make sure the decision follows the rules and is a good one. If you don't follow the rules and your parents or teachers find out, you might be punished.

In a similar way, big decisions that your parents, teachers, or politicians make must be legal. It's important to talk to your group members about what you can do to make sure your plan follows the rules or the law.

LEARNING IMPORTANT LAWS

Some of the most important laws are the ones that affect us every day. We have laws to keep us safe from harm. The same laws govern all American citizens, and it's very important that each citizen follows the law so other people aren't harmed and their rights aren't **jeopardized**.

The Constitution is the framework for laws in the United States, but it doesn't go into great detail about or include each law. You won't find traffic laws in the Constitution. Each state has its own vehicle and traffic laws.

Traffic laws protect us and prevent us from hurting other people. People have to obey the speed limits so they don't hurt other drivers or passengers. If a police officer catches someone breaking the law, then that person has to deal with the consequences. Laws also protect our rights.

When people disobey the speed limit, they put the lives of other drivers and passengers at risk. Legislators work very hard to create laws that keep citizens safe.

GROUP MEMBERS

One person can't make decisions for a group. This might make the other group members angry because their opinions weren't taken into consideration. Everyone's opinion is valuable. Although it might be impossible to include each person's opinion in the decisions, we have to think about these people's background. Why do they have this opinion? How can we reach a **compromise**? Remember that building consensus is helping the group members come to a decision they agree is a good one.

People's opinions often stem, in part, from their background. For example, a girl living in a small, rural town in the United States may have a different opinion about farming than a girl living in a big city. This is because they come from different backgrounds. In order to come to a consensus, people from these two areas may need to make compromises.

The **diversity** of a group makes it stronger. Each group member has **unique** opinions and perspectives that should be taken into consideration.

WHY OTHER OPINIONS MATTER

Your group members have had different experiences. This means that they may have different values and perspectives. The key to successfully making group decisions is taking these values and perspectives into consideration. In some cases, choices can be good for one person but not the group. Make sure you ask your group members what they think about the choices. Do any choices go against their personal values?

It is common for group members to make compromises when making decisions. This means that they may have to put some of their opinions aside to compromise with the opinions of the group. However, if this happens, the group needs to be very careful to make sure its decisions are doing more good than harm. What **impact** will this decision have on the people around them?

Sometimes we don't realize just how different we are from our peers. Their opinions are just as important as yours, so make sure to include them when making decisions.

THE IMPORTANCE OF CONSENSUS

Consensus isn't always necessary when making group decisions, but it does make things a lot easier. When a group agrees on a decision, no one will feel hurt. Including all group members makes them feel needed and valued, which makes the group stronger. Working toward a consensus requires **cooperation**.

While many groups will have a leader, building consensus can make group members feel as though everyone has some power. Most importantly, building consensus leads to stronger decisions that appeal to a larger number of people.

Ownership, or feeling that you have a stake in the decision, is an important aspect of building consensus. You can help your peers have ownership by asking them to share their ideas. Make sure each group member has a job and the power to make choices in the decision-making process. Talk with all group members about the plan for making the decision.

Think of the decision-making process as putting together a puzzle. Without all the pieces, the puzzle won't be complete. Strong group decisions are made up of many different points of view.

USING CONSENSUS IN PROBLEM SOLVING

Sometimes, people disagree strongly and a person called a mediator may have to come in to help them reach an agreement. When a mediator is brought in to help solve a problem, they follow certain steps. First, they identify the people who are disagreeing. Then they create a plan to help the group reach a decision. They define and **analyze** the problem and work with the group to come up with alternatives. The next phase requires the group to make the decision, finalize and approve the decision, and put the decision into place.

The United Nations (UN) is a group made up of representatives from a number of countries. The UN serves as a mediator to help solve political conflicts between countries when they come up, but it also practices preventative **diplomacy**. This means the UN takes action to prevent conflicts from happening.

In 2016, a UN Syrian **envoy** and members of the Syrian interior opposition met during Syria peace talks at the United Nations office in Geneva, Switzerland.

JURIES AND CONSENSUS

Conflicts are caused by a number of reasons. Most of these reasons can be sorted into eight groups: conflicting resources, conflicting styles, conflicting **perceptions**, conflicting goals, conflicting pressures, conflicting roles, different personal values, and inconsistent **policies**.

All these things can lead to conflict. Sometimes people break the law, which may lead to conflict. People involved in conflicts with the law may end up in court on trial. In some court cases, a jury discusses the evidence presented to the court by the disagreeing parties. After the jury has heard the findings of the court, jury members go into a private room to talk and reach a consensus. The jurors must voice their opinions and come to a group decision. In criminal cases, the jury usually needs to come to a **unanimous** decision, making a consensus even more important.

If a jury doesn't make a careful decision, then an innocent person could end up being punished for a crime they didn't commit.

WHEN CONSENSUS ISN'T POSSIBLE

Not all situations benefit from building consensus. If disagreeing parties don't have a common goal in the first place, a consensus won't work. Building consensus isn't truly compromise and it doesn't always lead to a unanimous vote. Each group member must be willing to voice an opinion and work with others to take elements of each point of view into account for a final decision.

This concept doesn't always fit with a group's plan of action. Some situations are better suited to making a decision through consensus building while some are better suited to voting. These are both ways to make a decision, but they can cause inequality. It often happens that people who have power, wealth, or high-ranking political positions control situations and their outcomes. This means that the needs of some group members are not taken into account.

Can you imagine having to build a consensus to select the next president of the United States? That would probably be impossible.

BUILDING CONSENSUS SUCCESSFULLY

Building consensus isn't always an easy process. When there are several points of view that need to be considered, making a decision can be tough. While the main goal of reaching a consensus is to make a decision, building strong relationships with your group members is also important. The consensus-building process can be a great way to establish trust between the members in a group.

Group members should listen to each person's point of view and consider it carefully.

Reaching a consensus involves several elements. First, the group members should have an understanding of what's involved in reaching a consensus. The members should understand what the process will involve and be willing to take part and cooperate. Each member of the group should feel comfortable sharing their point of view, free from other group members' judgment.

THE PROCESS

Reaching a consensus usually involves three stages. Discussion is the first stage. This is when the group members meet and talk about what they would like to accomplish. Everyone should be able to freely share their opinions and points of view, which may end up changing based on the opinions of the other group members.

The second stage is the proposal stage. At this point, the group comes up with a proposal, which states the topics agreed upon by the group and suggests options for reaching a final decision. The proposal is written down so that the group can revisit it in the future.

The final stage in reaching a consensus is the modification stage. During this stage, the proposal is tested and changes are made to it if necessary.

President Barack Obama, shown here on December 18, 2015, signs a $1.1 trillion spending package to fund the U.S. government. President Obama didn't agree with everything in the package, but he compromised to keep the American people's best interests in mind.

CONSENSUS IN PRACTICE

In the United States, presidential elections usually become a race between Democrats and Republicans. Members of these two political parties often have very different ideas about how the country should be governed. They are often unable to agree. The United States depends on its legislators to make decisions with the people's best interests in mind.

Many scholars believe that consensus in American politics doesn't exist. In the U.S. Congress, decisions are not reached by building consensus, but by a vote. In the same way, U.S. Supreme Court justices don't reach a consensus in court rulings. Supreme Court rulings are based on votes.

Reaching a consensus to benefit a large and diverse population is nearly impossible. However, this form of government is a better alternative to a dictatorship or some other form of government where the people have no say.

This political cartoon was featured in *Harper's Weekly* on May 28, 1904. It shows the Democratic donkey and the Republican elephant meeting each other on Wall Street. Both parties received financial support for their campaigns from Wall Street.

SMALL-SCALE CONSENSUS

Although it may seem like the U.S. government isn't capable of reaching a consensus on a large scale, it often does on a small scale. Both the Senate and the House of Representatives have committees to address specific issues. For example, the House Agriculture Committee deals with issues that affect the agricultural industry in the United States.

Committees and subcommittees help develop bills. They do this through lots of discussion, compromise, and consensus building. After they come to an agreement, the bill is discussed in the House or the Senate.

Legislators usually join committees that allow them to best serve the people of their state or congressional district. However, some legislators choose to join more powerful committees that allow them to have a larger impact on Congress's decisions. Even members of these powerful committees have to build consensus.

Secretary of Agriculture Henry Wallace (right), chairman of the Senate agricultural committee "Cotton Ed" Smith (left), and Howard R. Tolley of the Agricultural Adjustment Administration (center) discuss a farm bill in 1937.

CONSENSUS IN YOUR COMMUNITY

Getting involved in your community is a great way to make positive changes. If you—and other people—choose not to voice your opinion, it's possible no changes will be made.

Your education is one of the most important things at this point in your life. If you feel like something in your school isn't how it should be, you can attend a school board meeting to help adults understand your point of view.

At a school board meeting, members of the school board—a group of people from the community who are chosen by other community members—listen to the issues parents and other citizens bring up. The board may discuss the issue and come to a consensus. School board meetings are a great place to see consensus in action.

GLOSSARY

analyze (AA-nuh-lyze) To study something deeply.

compromise (KAHM-pruh-myz) An agreement in which each person or group gives up something in order to end a dispute.

cooperation (koh-ah-puh-RAY-shun) The act of working with others to get something done.

diplomacy (duh-PLO-muh-see) The work of keeping good relations between the governments of different countries.

diversity (dih-VUHR-sih-tee) The quality or state of having many different types, forms, or ideas.

envoy (AHN-voy) A representative sent by one government to another.

impact (IHM-pakt) A strong effect.

jeopardize (JEH-puhr-dyz) To place something in danger.

negatively (NEH-guh-tiv-lee) In a bad way.

perception (puhr-SEP-shun) A judgment resulting from awareness or understanding.

perspective (puhr-SPEK-tiv) Point of view.

policy (PAH-luh-see) A law that people use to help them make decisions.

unanimous (you-NA-nuh-muhs) Agreed to by all.

unique (yoo-NEEK) Special or different from anything else.

INDEX

PRIMARY SOURCE LIST

Page 25
President Obama approves spending package for 2016. Photograph. Created by Nicholas Kamm.
Created December 18, 2015. Washington, D.C.

Page 27
"What are you doing here?" Drawing. Created by William Allen Rogers. Published in *Harper's Weekly* on May 28, 1904.

Page 29
Senate Agricultural Committee works to frame a farm bill. Photograph. Created by Harris & Ewing.
Created November 17, 1937. Now kept at the Library of Congress Prints and Photographs Division
Washington, D.C.

WEBSITES